EARTH HEALER

A Library of the White Eagle Teaching

Earth Healer

USE YOUR OWN SPIRITUALITY IN THE SERVICE OF THE PLANET

Illustrated with photographs by Bruce Clarke

WHITE EAGLE PUBLISHING TRUST

NEW LANDS · LISS · HAMPSHIRE · ENGLAND

www.whiteaglepublishing.org

First published October 2010

© Text copyright,
The White Eagle Publishing Trust, 2010
Photography © copyright, Bruce Clarke, 2010

British Library CIP Data
A catalogue entry for this book can be had
from the British Library

ISBN 978-0-85487-214-5

Alongside this book, other White Eagle books which may be of interest to you are WHITE EAGLE ON THE GREAT SPIRIT, *in which White Eagle calls up memories of native American existence many years ago,* WHITE EAGLE ON FESTIVALS AND CELEBRATIONS, *which gives a deeper meaning to the seasons and moments of change and stillness that we celebrate during the year, and thirdly* PRAYER, MINDFULNESS AND INNER CHANGE, *which gives further 'processes' that help to change consciousness at the quiet personal level. Through all of his books you can develop your own practice and be part of a joyful and most rewarding cosmic process.*

Set in Monotype Spectrum and ITC Isadora
at the publisher and printed by
National Press, Amman, Jordan

Contents

EARTH HEALER

FOREWORD

How to Work with this Book

HOW CAN I be part of the healing of this planet? EARTH HEALER provides a beautiful and practical way to help, using positive thought, prayer and meditation. In it, the spirit teacher White Eagle combines the earth-healing wisdom of the Native Americans and the timeless Ancient Wisdom of the ages to provide the substance of a book that enables us to begin the process—right now.

'Live in spirit; live that spirit may manifest through you.' These words sum up the message of EARTH HEALER. White Eagle's response to the very great needs of the earth at the present moment is to create a change in consciousness that leads to a change in human behaviour—and not, as is so often proposed, a change in human behaviour which, if successful, might lead to a change in human consciousness. Addressing us from spirit, White Eagle teaches us the rules of spirit: rules that he offers us by way of simple, gentle guidance;

rules to live by, not rules to crush us.

Here is an example. Many years ago, White Eagle (who has always advocated as vegetarian a diet as circumstances allow) said that one day people would not eat meat for the reason that meat would simply not be sufficiently available. We have in this new century an economic situation in which some leading scientists point out that only abandonment of meat consumption will bring about the agricultural revolution required, partly to feed the earth's population, and partly to halt climate change. The lesson is that the rule of spirit that demands respect for life will always be the rule we have to live by, however long it takes us to realize this.

Indeed, White Eagle is rarely prescriptive. One very simple rule permeates his teaching, and it is to think constantly of the positive. Not foolishly: rather, to be positive by design because of another spiritual law, which is that all thought is creative, and while positive thought creates good, negative thought brings destruction. A key phrase of White Eagle's is simply, 'Create, create, create'. And in the case of our planet and its needs, there is nothing better we can do than to think positively and put into practice processes that change our consciousness and subtly change the consciousness of others.

The earth-healing process offered in this book is led by the power of thought, so that the very way you approach this book connects with the process. As our thoughts are filled with love and positive energy, so they help to bring healing to our planet. White Eagle's teaching helps us to understand the nature of the divine plan for our earth and to trust the processes and cycles of life. EARTH HEALER begins with a selection of teaching explaining the cycle of life and change which the earth is experiencing, and introducing the way in which our thoughts and prayers can make a real difference and help to heal the planet. The book is then divided into chapters representing separate processes linked to each of the traditional four elements—fire, earth, air and water. Through the prayers and visualizations in each chapter, White Eagle leads us spiritually through attunement to these four elements to bring healing to Mother Earth. The book ends with some suggestions for earth attunement and earth healing, including an actual service which groups could use.

You may wish simply to read this book right through, or dip into it to attune specifically to an element of life, or use it as a guide for prayer and daily meditation. You may wish to work your way through the elements, prayers and visualizations, or you may feel particularly drawn to use one of the photographs for meditation, or want to use one of the verbal symbols as a focus. However you work with it, and however much you retain intellectually, you have made a contribution to the life and beauty of our planet just by your imaginative generosity in connecting with it. Stay in your creative space as far as you can, not in your intellect. That way, you continue to create positive healing energy which will help to heal and protect the earth.

Occasionally, glimpses of White Eagle's own life on earth come through his words and remind us of a simple life of harmony. His vision throughout is one of the brotherhood of all life, one in which the action of every participant in the great scheme of life affects all the other participants. We have to go through the present process precisely to learn the need for this quality of brotherhood—and by brotherhood White Eagle does not mean a merely human interaction (and certainly not an exclusively male one!*) but rather an infinitely great connection between every possible level of life, demonstrated in the passage with the heading 'Brotherhood' on p. 35. Consciousness, he would say, applies to all creation, not just to one rather confused species. The White Eagle Lodge was founded to develop and increase the awareness of this sort of brotherhood and offers opportunities for training in brotherhood work.

As this book goes to press (late summer 2010), not only does the threat of climate change loom large, but a very particular tragedy has hit the Gulf of Mexico in the shape of the Deep-water Horizon oil spill. It is one of the biggest environmental 'disasters' in human history, and yet later generations of readers may, sadly, have their own examples to insert at this point. White Eagle's advice, even in such instances as these, is that there is no such thing as a disaster. There is suffering, there is destruction, certainly, but the very severity of the lesson learned by humanity may be exactly what the world needs to stimulate action which will, ultimately, be the tipping point to our salvation. The human response, the prayers said, the spiritual work done, may be transformational for whole generations. The passages in chapter two, point to this; they also point to 'a world-shattering awakening of the spirit'. That, too, will be for the good and not for waste or wanton destruction.

White Eagle's wisdom tells us that by creating peace and healing in ourselves, we can heal the world. Similarly, 'what you put into life, flows back in full measure'. Positive energy can move mountains. Just by beginning the earth-healing processes in this book, you are making a difference. Start today!

*There is no gender-free word that will stand in for 'brotherhood' without losing the moral quality that White Eagle wishes his word to have, or which avoids giving the impression that he is concerned only with human life. 'Brotherhood', to White Eagle, is a very powerful word denoting the sympathetic unity of all individuals, all species, all the realms of life and all the planes of life as well, and involving renunciation of selfish interests in its achievement.

EARTH HEALER

'I had a strange vision. I saw a great golden sun in the heavens, and it seemed to shine down upon a city, and all the buildings in the city appeared to be made of ice. They seemed to flash all colours in the sunlight, and it all looked very hard and frozen. Then suddenly, when it was least expected, the whole thing collapsed—simply melted right away and there was a fresh new earth. There were men and women on the earth ploughing and sowing, and it was a lovely day. The birds were singing and there was a feeling of healthfulness and simplicity and cleanliness. A new day had begun with the promise of a new life.'

White Eagle's channel, Grace Cooke
(She was known as 'Brighteyes' for her clear seeing)

This is the dawn of a new era for the world. The earth is ready to receive the fresh seed.

CHAPTER ONE

A New Era

IN PAST DAYS, men and women recognized the needs of the earth. Once, the wise ones, the masters of those days, studied the secrets of nature through observation of whatever grows, and through observation of the heavens and the planets. They discovered the influence of the planets and the sun upon the earth, upon themselves, and learned the secrets of the universe. They studied for long, long years the secrets of nature. They built temples of stone, which stood for the unshakeable, indestructible power of the sun; they worshipped the rising sun and made obeisance to the setting sun, for the light was the source of life and without the light there could be no life on earth. A vast concourse of people stood in silence with upraised arms to welcome the sunrise, and with the coming of the sun came also the spiritual power of their lives.

There were great things accomplished in those days, beyond the power of human beings today, for we know that ever since the earth was peopled it has passed through ages of varying consciousness. In those days people, by their knowledge of nature, were able to bring down the rain at the right time. They were able to sow their grain at the right time. They understood that they must be brotherly to other creatures and that their actions must be those of love. They would call on the nature spirits and be most thankful for their help, looking to them for the development of the seed, the growth of the crop and the nutriment of the harvest. They also treated the earth with kindness; they revered the earth because she was the womb of life, the Great Mother.

In this current cycle and in your generation, you are so clothed with civilization that you are shut away from this contact with the power of the earth. Humanity appears to be overwhelmed with material life and its problems; from our world we see that on your material plane life is noise, rush. There is no peace in the soul of the people. There is ignorance of the true values of life and the spiritual power is being dissipated. Humanity has again to learn the use of the senses; you need to learn how to make that true contact with the source of your creation and with universal life. You endeavour to contact this glorious spirit through your intellect—but in the time of our own life on earth we caught it directly through our five senses: a wonderful spiritual power and life-force.

We would assist you to open your senses, to raise your vibrations above the material earth, above the heavy and depressing conditions which hang over your planet like a dense fog.

If you could see from above, you would see a heavy fog, like a pall, over your nations. It is particularly dense over the cities. Earth … the very name sounds muddy and dark! People are bowed down in the mists and gloom, though they hardly understand why—but the yearning for light is still deep within you, and the power behind all matter is the greatest thing in life, is the source of your life. Your soul longs for this unknown comfort and strength and source of truth.

May your eyes instead be opened. May your senses realize the beauty of the unseen world about you!

If only people would raise their vision upwards and penetrate the mists of their own heavy thoughts, they would see something so beautiful that they would be filled with deep thankfulness…. They would see into the world of spirit, into a world of infinite beauty, of the perfection of life, the perfection of nature. They would see into a world of perfect harmony, of perfect spiritual law, where the people are living in conditions of inestimable happiness and joy and peace of heart; where the earth is healed. The brothers and sisters of old had the secret.

If you seek to help humanity or the animal

kingdom or nature's growth, any plant or tree or flower, seek within your heart the light … for this is something you can direct, by your thoughts and by your love and devotion, to God's creatures. Live in spirit; live that spirit may manifest through you. Live in spirit that you may call forth from your brother and your sister the spirit which lies so deeply buried; and the harvest of the sowing of the seed of spirit shall be lasting happiness and healing for the earth!

The task lies before each one to sow the seeds in order that the pure spirit may grow and flourish on the earth.

CHAPTER TWO

The Ways in which the World Grows

AT CERTAIN seasons and times, there is a sense of waiting. You may get the sense that nature itself is waiting for a world initiation, waiting to burst forth in glorious manifestation. Nature itself awaits the world of light. But before that manifestation comes to the earth there is a short season of apparent darkness, silence, expectancy. Before great change, there is this moment of waiting, and then comes the great trial, the testing.

The world is passing through this testing, and as individuals, you too are passing through such a period of testing. You look out upon your world, you see its chaotic conditions, and you note that human life appears to be storm-tossed. You wonder what will be the end of your current concerns about human life. Remember always, that there is a wise purpose and good is coming out of what may appear to be negative. When the earth is in darkness, when the thoughts of millions of people are downcast and dark, you become the channels through which the Great Spirit can send through to humanity the blazing spiritual light.

You all know that the planet has arrived

at a critical stage. The earth is going through a crucifixion at the present time, when all that is unwanted, all that is waste matter, is gradually being dissolved away. Yet behind every department of earthly life, there are greater minds working for the evolution of the planet. The great ones have the very crust of the earth in their care and under their wise direction and power. Angels are moving up and round and about, directing rays of spiritual life-force to the earth, so there is bound to be a certain amount of disturbance on the earth—changing of tides and currents, along with rain and floods. This is the need of the earth: the planet must be purified, glorified and perfected, and therefore at the present time and for a little time to come, the earth will need powerful healing.

So when you see even what appears to you to be catastrophe, bear in mind that the Master Mind is at work, even as a gardener is when he carries his pruning knife; and although you may have intense powers of sympathy, remember that the masters and the angelic ones have a far deeper sympathy and love than you for all who suffer. Simply, we ask, do not think that this suffering means the world is deteriorating. On the contrary, the world is being stimulated by rays of light, and although its suffering does seem cruel to you, the very suffering is working out something. The events that sometimes cause you so much grief happen for one grand purpose, which is to cleanse and to clear the earth, in exactly the same way as your physical body, when it has ceased to be useful to the spirit, is discarded and its form is changed, although the real you lives on. The disruptions and conflicts on your earth upon which you look with sorrow are really good, because they are breaking up crusts of materialism and injustice and cruelty.

You are on the verge of a great awakening on your earth. I am going to say a world-shattering awakening … a world-shattering awakening of the spirit. The earth is shaking like a great animal which is giving birth to its young. Birth pangs are painful and the earth is suffering from birth pangs now. When you get depressed and you despair for the world, remember that before there can be a new building and new growth there must be a clearing of the land, there must be a ploughing of the earth, a cleansing of the soil. When a physical condition is finished, it has to be cleared away.

Remember nonetheless that although the form of some physical part of the whole is changed, the very atoms, the very particles of that physical earth, are continuing to do a good work in Mother Earth. Nothing dies; certainly not the spirit and not even the physical or material atoms. They change their form, and out of the dead ashes arises a new life.

Labour

Try to surrender yourselves in the birth pangs of the new way of life, for the present time is the time of human labour before the birth of a glorious age of new material and spiritual power. You are witnessing the karma of the world working itself out. Science may think it all happens according to certain natural laws; yet this is not the whole truth: there is an intelligence at work behind the happenings and catastrophes which take place at different periods of the earth's history. These happenings occur by the wisdom and the will of the great lords of karma.

Again, it is like what happens to the physical body. Sometimes the physical body suffers through disease; but we assure you that there is also a beneficent holy power that comes to cleanse humanity, comes to cleanse the earth from all disease and pollution. All things move forward for the cleansing and the saving of the earth. Old conditions are being broken up and cleared away to make room for a fresh influx of life which is to come on the physical plane, and this life brings with it pure sweet air from those higher realms of life, which blesses all earthly life, and all humanity.

You look around you in your world and you become disappointed by the disputes and misunderstandings between people and the conflict between the races and faiths of the world. You bemoan revelations of the things that are happening on your earth and forget that side by side with that darkness is always the angel of light. So we say, do not give way to despondency when you read or hear about war and disagreement on the earth plane! It is all a sign of growth. Even when you see apparently terrible things happening, do not be pessimistic. We know that there are troubles in your land, whichever it may be, indeed all over the earth—but we see beyond your physical sight and we see a wonderful unfoldment.

'God proposes, man disposes', says your proverb. Yet remember that disposal just as much as proposal and creation comes under divine law. There is a continual absorption and dissolution as well as creation. When seen rightly, both these aspects of life are working together to bring growth and evolution. You cannot stay the progress of evolution; and what you are witnessing on the earth today is growth and change, and you must welcome it, not try to stop it. It will not be stayed; it will come on the earth, and the sooner humanity recognizes this, the sooner will we all know happiness and health, the sooner will we enjoy the blessings and the glories.

There is a breaking up at the moment of the powers of ignorance and darkness, a breaking up of the solid crust of complacency. There is a unification coming, a breakthrough in the dark clouds that have for so long been in the sky round this earth plane. The light is now shining, gently falling upon the earth ... and it is certain that the light is working out its purpose.

You are Light!

Realize that in the process of life there must come change, change of form. Think of a bud, and the growth of the bud into a beautiful rose. See now the petals of the rose unfolding as the sunlight and the dew falls upon them. Gaze upon that dew-drenched flower. You might almost say that it is weeping—but tears are refreshing and are cleansing.

See through the happenings on your earth, and see beyond them the release of light and love and truth in the heart of man and woman. You may be anxious about humanity, about your own country, about the planet and about all the conditions and the threatening happenings in the world; yet we tell you that good is increasing all the time. You may not like the old order passing, but we impress this upon you all, regarding suffering: never cross your bridge before you come to it, and if and when you come to it you will be carried across it with great power and love. You will live to see some wonderful revelations and progress on earth, and they are coming very rapidly.

Accept with a peaceful mind the changes and upheavals, seeing in all these things the gradual permeation of the light. The light is bringing changes, and you must move forward with these changes, knowing in your spirit that all things work together for good. Do not concern yourselves unduly with the superficial effects on the earth, but concern yourselves wholly with the God-purpose in life.

At this moment there is an outpouring of spiritual life-force. Let yourselves receive these rays. We will liken this to a preparation for the next step; we ourselves can feel the outpouring of this great spiritual power of peace and wisdom, thus quickening the consciousness of humanity to desire wisdom, peace, brotherhood and love towards all creatures, particularly the animal kingdom. This spiritual outpouring is a preparation for people individually and for the whole earth, a preparation to receive the next outpouring. That spirit in humanity has to grow, to be awakened, to be fostered.

Look out for signs of the spiritual progress of humanity. Among you there is so much concentration upon what is called evil; too much concentration upon fear and negativity. When you see what you call darkness and evil, or sin and crime, by their side is exactly the same outburst of light. Therefore do not bemoan what you call crime and evil. Light and darkness work together.

Sometimes the earth is referred to as a dark planet, as this is a very dark world in comparison with those realms of light and beauty above. So the purpose of life on this earth planet is that spirit, your spirit, will shine within the darkness. Always there is this penetration of the one source, the one principle of all life, to the earth itself. That one principle is light, and it is called love. It permeates every sphere and every plane. That secret power is the same power as the light that creates all beauty in life, and humanity contains the secret.

Buried still in the earth is the ancient light and its power can only be released spiritually. This light radiates through the whole of life; it is manifested through every plane, right from the highest spiritual plane down through the mental, the astral, the etheric, right to the physical. When we get to earth, it manifests even through the natural animal kingdom and the mineral. All the time we are drawing from the one source of truth. The same light is all around, is shining in nature, even in the animal kingdom and the mineral kingdom.

The human race is not very evolved today but it will become great again when this secret power has been released and the whole vibration of the earth thereby raised. Do not forget, in concentrating upon this light, that the same light shines in every living soul. You are here, you are light; and you have to shine out through the darkness! If your light is used for the upliftment and blessing of the earth, it will bring to the world the golden age.

Part of a Greater Life

DWELL ON your creative thoughts. Become part of them; become part of it, the first great cause. The greatest work that any man or woman can be engaged in is the work of consciously using the power which saves and blesses and brings heaven on earth; the opportunity is one which may not come to you again for many lives.

As you gaze into the sky you will see countless millions of stars, and in this object lesson you will realize that you are part of a vast whole; you are part of invisible, eternal and infinite life, and that invisible life goes on and on and on. These ideals are slowly being born. Once you recognize that you are part of the infinite, universal life, you will know that you cannot hurt anything—any part of creation—without injuring yourself; you cannot violate Mother Earth without hurting yourself because you are part of everything that lives, and everything that lives is part of yourself.

Remember the spider's web, a drawing together of myriad gossamer lines. Remember also how easily the spider's web is broken and how very quickly the little spider repairs it. This also is taking place in the great, grand universe in which you live and move, not only on the earth but in spheres of spiritual life, and in the soul world.

Great cosmic events are shaping the destinies of millions and are shaping and reshaping the surface of the earth. This little planet has been passing through great trial and tribulation and its humanity is beginning to emerge from a chrysalis state. And you know what happens to the insect then: it spreads its wings and it flies!

This has happened in past 'golden ages' on this planet. Earth's humanity has to pass through many changes and pass the cycles of growth and unfoldment. It is very slow; at every stage of development things happen to it—but take heart, you are on the upward leg, moving towards your goal. You have to use your light in the physical life to transmute the heavy atoms of the physical earth. Then will the light and power imprisoned within the very stones of the earth be released. You will see not destruction, but construction, a wonderful lightening of the human burden on earth. Humanity will struggle for a time in the mists of materialism and selfishness, but the light will shine through like the sun breaking through fog; and you will see the light shedding rays all over the earth.

You will see over the earth the spirit of truth and goodness and beauty; the present very hard conditions will pass and in the spring days you will enjoy the blessing of the warm sunshine and flowers. This is what you are working to bring into the consciousness of humanity—the real life around it and the life as it should be lived on this earth planet. We have to make an effort for the good, the true and the beautiful to dominate—and then the whole earth will change. You will find your own life travelling very steadily towards that golden, *golden* world and towards the life which will be so beautiful.

THE WAYS IN WHICH THE WORLD GROWS

Have no doubt at all that your individual thought can affect the whole world. It is like a light passing from one mind to another to illumine the planet.

CHAPTER THREE

The Power of Thought

WE WANT to impress on you the great importance of preparing yourselves as channels for the beauty of the light to spread over the whole earth. People are needed by the earth; the planet needs you, as an individual. However small and insignificant you may feel, the time has now come for you to work for the purification of the earth plane. What all the world needs is light, love, goodwill, and you, as a human being, can be a channel for this.

There is so much confusion on your earth, so much confusion now between the countries and the peoples of the world. The mists caused by the thoughts of humanity are very dense and you all feel the oppression of these mists. But you are courageous and have set your course, and you go straight forward. We would have you hold the picture of peace and a perfect life of harmony, brotherhood, goodwill; a life of co-operation, not of selfishness. All your work can be summed up in one phrase: 'to overcome egotism and selfishness'. And if, with your help, we can assist those on earth to a state of brotherly love and understanding and a desire to help each other, then indeed you will be accomplishing a great work.

Remember that you are the builders. Your love and your positive thought are a creative power for good, for beauty, for truth, in your body, in your life and in the whole world.

And so we ask you to create in your mind the image of a perfect world, a perfect land. The way for human beings to restore the perfect life on this planet, to restore harmony and brotherhood, is to hold humanity and the earth in a perfect thought, a thought of harmony, beauty, brotherly love and wholeness or healthiness. The power of thought is the power of creation, and we are endeavouring to teach you the creative power of thought, the power of good thought or God thought. The whole of creation is held in God's thought, in the thought of the infinite Spirit.

How can we find earthly words to help you comprehend this fundamental truth? One day you will understand how subtle is the power that can manipulate soul substance and physical matter: the power of thought. When you concentrate upon an ideal or upon a form, very quickly that form is created. When you concentrate upon an idea, it brings that idea into existence. Now it may be that the thought is weak—in which case the creation will be weak, and scarcely formed; but if your thought is strong, inspired by the spirit—particularly the spirit of love—the thought very quickly becomes a reality. Remember that you have within your heart this almighty power.

It will come to you as you practise good thought, positive thought. It can save you and it can recreate you and your life and your work; you can affect the lives of your fellow beings by putting into their minds the right thought, God thought. *You can change the very atoms of the physical earth by thought.*

We told you on one occasion that the thoughts of one good man or woman, directed with power and goodwill and love, could affect the thoughts of thousands. An individual's thought is externalized in his or her world; the collective thought of a nation produces the state of that nation. Good thought, God thought, positive good thought, works.

It is our work, and yours, to think positively and always concentrate positive good upon conflict and cruelty. Your thoughts, even your speech, your attitude to this healing of the earth, can help so much, because it is while you are in a physical body and your mental body is being directed by your brain that humanity can receive tangible help, close help.

With those in the physical body, a tremendous amount depends upon their thought, their attitude towards their surroundings and the conditions in the physical life. You have the power within you to free yourselves from the bondage of material and physical life. And once again we ask every person to hold fast to this fundamental truth—the power of your individual thought, and of your speech and actions.

We have said to you on former occasions that if you will transfer your thoughts from physical matter to spiritual life, you will solve your problems. This is a truth. Do not think about physical conditions or problems of the earth. Think about God and you will be with God.

You are not alone. There are many wise ones watching, inspiring, guiding. Do not think you are carrying the responsibility of humanity's right living, right action and right thinking. The only responsibility you are carrying is for yourselves.

It comes down to this, that every single person has an immense opportunity to send forth the thought of God. Just think of God and give God the opportunity to work through the physical life; and this applies to all the aspects of your life on earth. If the light is generated and sent forth, you are acting with all the power that God has given you to assist your earth companions to respond to and absorb the light which is being sent to them. Good thought, God thought, can raise the whole life of humanity.

Thought-Pollution

You have a divine and perfect mind. Bring this mind into action. The charge comes to you, to eradicate polluted thought. There is much talk about pollution, pollution of the earth, the waters of the earth, and of the air. Think for a moment of the pollution of the air by noise and what this does to the air spirits, driving them away, disturbing the work which has been given to them by the Great Spirit. Think of the pollution of physical states of life—of the water, of the earth, and the air—but the very heart and centre of your work for the planet must be the cleansing of thought pollution.

You do not know the power of your thoughts on your bodies, in your homes and on your world. When you think negatively you are contributing to the pollution of all life, you are contributing to the negative, heavy atmosphere of thought that holds people down.

We repeat, you have a divine mind, as well as a mind of earth. See the perfect life—the life that we know in the world of spirit, a life where

EARTH HEALER

all work together for the good of the whole. This is the creative goodness, which you can project into the world: first of all in your own life and in your own family, and then in the community, in your own country. When you work like this, giving your heart and your mind to the service of your human brethren or any of the kingdoms of life, human, animal, vegetable, mineral, you are contributing the creative power of the Great Spirit. You, as an individual, are assisting in the recreation of the earth and humanity. You are helping forward and upward the spiritual evolution of creation. The power of the Great Spirit within you can recreate your body and your life; it can recreate this planet earth, which is now undergoing a tremendous recreation itself.

You can receive and can give to the world—to your world, the one in which you live your daily life. We wait on you and your thoughts of purity, of loving kindness to all creation—to humanity, the animal kingdom and the nature kingdom, which includes the earth itself and the rocks and the sea and the little creatures on the seashore. We assure you that with your thoughts you can enfold all creation in pure love…. This love is protective, and it is so important for it to be sent out from you.

The Power of Love

Think of this: love is ever constructive, ever progressive. The love vibration is what holds all things in place. It is important for it to radiate at the human and physical level, because at this level all creatures who are also on the physical level of life can be reached, on that physical level. Concentrate upon love—love everywhere—and you will be doing more to help your planet than any form of earthly legislation can accomplish, because spiritual knowledge will flood the earth to preserve its equilibrium. The power of love will automatically right that which is in disorder.

In your ordinary physical life, if you go into a darkened room, you immediately switch on the light, and this is what we want you to do now in this misty, darkened atmosphere of the world. The mind of earth is barren and dark and confused; it is anxious and it grows weary. You are a channel for the light, the light of the Great Spirit, the power of love in all human hearts. You must learn to apply that light before anything else in your life, before everything that is done—individually or nationally or internationally.

It is simple—but not easy. The earth silently calls to you to be untiring in your efforts to project the light, to send forth the light in positive form. The light overcomes all darkness: always remember this. We tell you to have no fear, nor anxiety, but to work and work and work to project the light to heal the planet.

And in this way, most beautiful work is going on all over your world. Never concentrate on negative things or dark forces, for in the light they do not exist. We would bring you encouragement and hope by telling you that the human kingdom is now building, that this earth planet is moving towards the spiritual. It is so slow, the progress of spiritual becoming, but the world is moving steadily and surely forwards; more and more you will find that power sweeping through your heart and your life, recreating, reshaping, beautifying, glorifying your earthly life.

We see, as you must see in due time, the progress being made in human life, the lessons which are most surely being learned. Countless people on earth are doing what they can to help others. This love is always at work—this light, this tenderness, this understanding one for another.

Oh, there is so much good on your earth! Life is not meant to be a life of struggle and pain and sorrow; it is meant to be a glorious thing. We who work in the temple above, in the golden world of spirit, see such devotion in the people's hearts. Maybe they do not work quite as you work, but so many work unceasingly to help others and uplift life. They may not know with their minds, but they know in their hearts, and they long to help and uplift other people.

So far as earthly conditions are concerned, we assure you most earnestly and sincerely that valuable lessons are being learned by humanity all over this planet—valuable spiritual lessons, the learning of which will eventually bring the golden age upon earth. No matter how difficult the conditions on your earth are at the moment, have confidence, for you are moving forward and upward. Humanity is learning the lesson of brotherly love, of consideration; learning that all human beings are children of God. So take heart, and you will see the light triumph. The light will shine steadily. You think too much about the confusion and the tragedies in the world today; but the tragic

events are breaking up and dispersing the old unwanted ways of life, and humanity is being shown that the only way to live happily, joyously and healthily is to love. A vision of the light pouring upon the trees, bare of leaf but just showing tiny buds upon their branches, is a symbol which all might do well to note. It is a symbol of promise.

Dwell on Beauty

We have another very important message for you: we ask you to concentrate on beauty. We have a very good reason for saying this. The earth is grey, and at times there is a dark mist on your earth. We won't say any more, just say there is a dark mist—and there is so much ugliness on earth. There is ugliness of speech, of sound, of buildings—ugliness in so many departments of life. What we all have to do is to create beauty.

Beauty is a spiritual food—beauty of form; beauty in nature, in Mother Earth; beauty in colour, in movement, in music, in thought, in expression. All these aspects of beauty are so important. By your concentration upon beauty—in your surroundings, in yourself, in your thoughts—try to convey beauty into the lives of others around you. See perfection, ignore all the ignorant chatter.

When you work from the spirit you are creating beauty and helping humankind to absorb and to express beauty, in all its forms. You who have been trained to meditate see beauty because you are working from your innermost spirit. Imagine the world of spirit; think of the beauty of colour and form and sound. Think of the music, the harmony of the spheres. When you are attuning yourselves to the higher life, to the spirit world, you should always hold a picture which is beautiful.

The most ideal subjects for meditation are to be found in nature. You may visualize the mountains, the still lake or pool in the temple gardens in the spirit world, or the beautiful garden of flowers. All these natural scenes have an effect upon your soul. They bring you into rapport with the Great Spirit. In the infinite and eternal garden you will see angelic forces, forms with human faces in colours unmatched on earth, still and peaceful—continually giving, giving, giving help, pouring love and wisdom upon creation. We suggest that in your meditations you always concentrate, as far as you are able, upon the Great Spirit, and then upon the beauty of nature.

This form of meditation is very simple, but the more you repeat it, the more it will help you in your work. If you begin by concentrating on beauty in all its forms, we assure you that you are not neglecting suffering, or the inequalities of life. Give from your heart the perfect love and see your beautiful world cleansed of all pollution. See the beautiful earth used by humanity according to the law of God—humankind giving back to the land what they receive from it.

Do you not feel, as we speak, the harmony of this circle of life? No one can form any idea of the grandeur and the beauty of the infinite scheme. There is no such thing in all creation as splendid isolation; no separation between any form of life, but all is blended in one harmonious whole. What appears to be error, evil, destructiveness, has behind it the great power, wisdom and love outworking through the whole plan, bringing good out of apparent evil, guiding and linking up every form of life.

This is a grand thought: all is working together for good and nothing can harm the one who loves goodness and truth. You are increasing the light over the whole of this planet. Always be ready to go forward with the power of the spirit that enters your soul; go forward in faith to enter into eternal peace and joy and happiness, and when this planet becomes a planet of light, which it will, it will become a shining star in the heavens.

You are on a path of eternal progress. You will enter into the golden world of God.

Brotherhood

One who has realized his sonship or her daughtership to the Father–Mother God instantly recognizes relationship to all of God's creation. This means that he or she goes about life with eyes and heart wide open. The true brother or sister of life recognizes the beauty in nature, in bush and tree and flowers and grass; in the little insects; in a beautiful building; in the symmetry and beauty of the trees; even in a piece of wood he or she instantly sees the beauty of the grain. If she looks at an animal she notices the marking in its coat, the whiteness of its teeth, the brave cheery glint in its eyes. All these things she instantly sees. He goes into the woods and his ears are open to the orchestra of nature—the birdsong, the gentle breeze rustling the leaves of the trees. He looks at the sky—which may be grey, but may also be blue and sunlit—and feels a kinship. She enters a building and notices every detail of comfort that has been provided, the grace and beauty of the building itself. He thinks of the souls of men and women who have contributed their best to bring about this end.

The Great White Spirit: immortal, invisible, infinite, eternal love, from whom all creatures derive life.

CHAPTER FOUR

Preparation: the Great Spirit, Source of Creation

OUR NATIVE American brothers and sisters learned, through their observation of nature and by living in natural conditions, some of the secrets of the invisible power which is called the Great White Spirit, or Great Spirit. All the aspiration of the people went out to this invisible Great Spirit, which they recognized in their hearts in all its manifestations of life: in the growing corn, in the falling rain, in the warm sunshine, in the trees and the wild flowers.

They blessed the roots and the seeds with the light of the Great White Spirit before they were planted; they directed the light into the earth. In all the natural life of their world they recognized the Great White Spirit everywhere as a giver of life, a giver of food, a source of light and power. They learned to accept all as being good, for they understood that the Great White Spirit was in supreme command. They knew that the Great White Spirit sent forth the command, and the stars and planets and the great planetary beings and angels, right down to the little nature spirits, obeyed the command.

This was not only a Native American tradition; many ancient races did this. The ancient people were more attuned to the forces of nature than you are today, and they were more attuned to the spiritual forces behind matter. These people, because of their simplicity, were more open to what we call 'the light'. Yet you are all channels for this light, for the spirit— for you are spirit just as much as they, part of the Great White Spirit. The spiritual light pours like a broad river through many channels, or like a wide beam from a searchlight of a strength you cannot conceive with your earth mind. The Great White Spirit is forever pouring out light upon humanity.

So much work lies all around you, waiting to be done. Part of that work is to open the eyes of people on earth to the true values of life and to an understanding of eternal life and of the Great White Spirit. The Great White Spirit *is*

the love and the light of the new age of brotherhood and spiritual life unfolding in human beings and all creatures, and in the very substance of the earth itself.

Never forget this. You have to live your life so that you gradually expand your consciousness to embrace the heaven world, the golden world of spirit. The more you open yourselves to it, the closer it will come, and so transform your life. It will bring love into your heart, and harmony and happiness into all human life.

We would try to lay aside the lower mental covering and rise to the Great White Spirit, praying for the blessing of the inflow of love, wisdom and power. You will see change in your own country and in many other countries. The Great White Spirit is watching over His–Her children and guiding them through the darkness into a better state, a better world, a better kind of life.

Visualization

Will you endeavour to withdraw from the planes of earth, and imagine that you are in spirit, that you are on the summit of a mountain, far removed from the rush and the turmoil of the city? Upon this high place you are raised nearer to the Great White Spirit….

You find yourself outside all the limitations of the flesh and the physical plane. You will see with clear vision new beauty in form, and particularly in nature's form—in the grass and the flowering bush and the majestic tree, in the earth and the sky and the water and the life within the water. You will feel and see that you are part of these. You are not separate, you are a part of all this beautiful life of nature, the Great White Spirit. You see an intensity of colour, a beauty of form, a sweetness of perfume. You experience a new clarity of hearing. You hear the music of the spheres.

Look always for the spirit behind or within all form. Become en rapport with the Great Spirit in everything you see. Realize it in the air you breathe, in the water you drink and in the water in which you bathe. See it in the sky, in the winds, in the air. See it in the fire; see the little fire spirits. Sense it in the beauty of the plants and the flowers and the fruit. It will create harmony in you and beauty in your lives, for you will have realms revealed to you that you do not know and of which you cannot even dream.

Prayers of the Spirit

Great White Spirit of the great open spaces, the mountaintops and the quiet, peaceful valleys; Great White Spirit of nature and of the heavens above the earth and of the waters beneath; Great White Spirit of eternity, infinity: we are enfolded within Thy great heart. We rest our heart upon Thy heart. Great Father and Mother God, we love, we worship Thee. We resign all into Thy loving keeping, knowing that Thou art love, and all moves forward into the light. Amen.

Let us pray to the Great White Spirit, to the Source of life, to the sun, the light, the truth. Unto the Great Spirit we give our humble love and service. May the peace of the great open prairie enfold us; in this deep, deep peace may we know Thee. May this earth planet be caught up in Thy glory. Amen.

O Great White Spirit, who art in all things visible and invisible, from whom all life cometh; Thou who art the song of the birds, the perfume of the flowers; Thou who art the sweet music of the wind, Thou who art all beauty and truth, all wisdom; Thou who art to be found only in the deep tranquillity of spirit—O Divine Love, we pray that we may become aware of Thee in ourselves and in our companions, in all life. Amen.

The heart of the golden sun is the source of all our strength.

CHAPTER FIVE

Fire: The Sun

WHEN PEOPLE in ancient days were spiritually quickened, they worshipped the sun, not merely because it was the life-giver of the physical life, but because they saw beyond and behind the physical manifestation a spiritual power and knew its true origin. The sun worshippers knew the spiritual meaning of that physical representation of the light, which was the illumination, the life-giver of their world.

The physical sun is a reflection of the spiritual sun. Life in every form is created from the sun. Even as your heart is the centre and lifegiver of your body, the power which motivates your physical body, so the sun is like the heart of the universe. The core of all mysteries lies in the descent of the earth life from the sun. Never regard the sun above as merely a molten mass of fire, but think of it as a glorious reflection of divine light.

Long ago, the ancient peoples were taught and understood that they were touching the very heart of life and the secret of power when they opened themselves to the sun. They knew at that moment they were not only receiving into their being, each one, the radiation of the Solar Logos, but that they were being strengthened and purified. They breathed in the Light—which was actual life-force, the purifier, perfector and glorifier of life. And this knowledge of the power and the life emanating from the light was handed down through the ages, from generation to generation.

Remember that you too hold within yourself that solar force. It is within you, buried deeply, and lies there sleeping. An outpouring of golden light reaches you—if you can open your heart to this blessing. It is like a spark which bursts into fire. Then will come the rising of this solar force into your etheric body, your physical body, into all your bodies and every centre. These centres will commence pulsating and will open as a flower opens to the sun. You will be recreated on every plane of being. We know that this creative power can and will—and does—consume all inharmony. This mighty Presence, this great Light, is unstoppable. No inharmony can live in that Light.

Try to realize the power of that glorious sun light. You enjoy the sunshine on your earth; you bask in the sunshine and say how lovely it is, but it is only the slightest gleam in comparison with the spiritual Sun. So in your meditation we ask you to rise above the limitation and the darkness of the earth plane, into that world of the light of the Sun, and to open your inner vision and see the glory of the Sun's creation in that higher world. Live in it, in spirit; breathe it into your being. It is power, it is life, it is truth. Breathe in the divine life, absorb into your being the radiance of the great Sun, and go about your life and your work in physical matter warm and radiant in the Sun, the life-giver.

Sun Prayers

We raise our faces to the glory of the sun. O Gracious Spirit, we bless and thank Thee for Thy blessing, which comes as a stream of light and happiness perfecting the life in us. Amen.

We turn our faces to the sun, the source of all life, and we give thanks, Gracious Spirit, for Thy blessing. May it remain in our hearts as peace and love and service. May the blessing of the sun, the Source of the whole of humanity, be upon us now. Amen.

Our thanks, O Great Spiritual Sun, for the blessings and warmth of your light. We pray for your care and healing to purify and nurture our earth and the world of nature. Amen.

Visualization

Be still. In the golden evening light, you are carried into the sun temple. All your thoughts that reach that height bring back to you the power of creating new life in your body, in your soul, from the Creator.

The power of thought takes you anywhere. Call it imagination if you like, but see beyond your imagination into the glory of God's heaven, because it is only by your heavenly vision and your heavenly hearing, that you will reach that Temple of the Sun.

See the vast plain in the centre of the circle of mountains crowned with the golden sun, where countless souls are gathered. Look, and you will see a vast concourse. You will see the heavens open and the light streaming down, and you will see the great sun altar, upon which the divine fires eternally burn. The fire is called into being by the command of the Creator of all life. You can feel its radiation, and from the centre of this fire, burning on the golden altar you will both see and hear the music of the spheres and you will interpret these spiritual sounds.

Now there appears in the heart of the sun–fire the form of the Great Spirit, the source of creation. With this vision there come countless other stars and planets. We are looking right into the solar system, right into the cosmos. All are one in this vast panorama of pulsating life. Now we see the reflection of the sun on other worlds and on the moon. We want you to become aware in your souls of this cosmic universe…. Breathe and live in the consciousness of this infinite and eternal cosmic universe.

At this moment, try to feel in your heart, in your whole being, the confidence of peace—peace and goodwill. You must hold this confidence if you are to develop your spiritual strength; you must continually work for the healing of humanity, and you will see the threatening clouds that hang over humanity disperse. The sun will shine again and you will see, as we can see, an ever-increasing desire on your earth for peace, brotherhood and goodwill.

A Golden Rose

Imagine a rose, a flaming golden rose, perfect in shape and colour, opening its petals to the spiritual sun whose light falls upon it. Try to put yourselves *en rapport* with that rose. Inhale the spiritual perfume, absorb the delicacy of its life, its aura. It will raise you far above the earth into a world of silence, peace, love, truth.... This is the symbol of purity: absolute purity, love untainted by the earth. The love of God is symbolized by the rose, the perfect flower, which holds in its creation both aspects of life: light and darkness, joy and pain. Both qualities alike contain the sweet fragrance which must balance and perfect the human soul.

We suggest that you concentrate upon that symbol. Meditate upon the symbol of the Great Spirit—visualize the perfect rose, the symbol of love. If you have a physical rose to look at, look at it with your physical eyes first and then close them and hold the picture in your mind. You will find that just doing this will have an effect upon you and upon your emotions, and you will feel a sense of peace and beauty.

Give, give as you have received. As you feel this love, this sweetness, this happiness that the fire of love brings when it opens like the rose in your heart, give. Give to the brother and the sister by your side, to those in your home and in the communities in which you work. Give to the earth the fragrance of the rose.

We know of no symbol so perfect as the rose to convey to the mind the love of the Great Spirit.

⋆

In this Aquarian Age, where the intellect tends to become a god, it is so necessary for the fragrance of the rose to be continually projected onto the mental plane, so that those who are engrossed in mental pursuits may occasionally catch the waves of perfume and fragrance. Now, when you can touch that part of your consciousness where the rose lies, a place of surrender of self, you will inhale truly the perfume of the rose. If you can catch that radiation—if you can just receive it into your heart—you will indeed receive a heavenly blessing of healing for all life.

So we ask you to remember at all times to seek to absorb the beauty and perfume of the golden rose. Just one blazing golden rose!—we bring to you this spiritual gift. If you could see it with clear vision you would see the light and the perfume rising within it, as well as the rose radiating its light and fragrance and beauty all around. It projects the light to attract the Light; and the rays of the Great Spirit, of the Supreme Being, fall gently like sunlight upon that rose, for it represents the fire of divine love.

Prayers of the Rose

As we rise upon the spiral of the divine life-force, may our hearts expand with love towards all humanity. May all selfishness fall away, may our hearts overflow with love for the world. As we approach the heart of the rose, the divine Great White Spirit, may our hearts be filled with perfect, pure love, the fragrance of the rose, the love for the earth and for the world of nature. Amen.

We thank the Great Spirit for life, for all that it brings to us of joy, knowledge and wisdom. We pray that the consciousness of Thy love will be our companion for ever. May love and beauty, truth and wisdom accompany Thy children on earth, that they may overcome all bitterness and all war, all cruelty. Amen.

O Gracious Spirit, may the fragrance of the rose bathe the earth, that fear and suffering may cease and beauty and peace return. Amen.

Visualization

See now, the rose is growing in the temple garden in spirit, and you are walking in this garden. Imagine the rose, that blazing golden rose, opening wide to the sunlight and forming an immense temple….

Let us go into the heart of the Temple of the Rose, and let us touch the vibrations and the substance of the sunlight, the petals of gentle golden light. Feel yourself enfolded by the golden petals of the Rose Temple….

Upon the altar in spirit you will find a rose for you. Take your rose and lay it on your heart, and absorb its fragrance. Visualize the rose there upon your heart. Meditate upon it, inhale the perfume with your spiritual senses. May the fragrance of the rose beautify your soul, and may you learn to let the rose bloom for you upon the cross of the material life….

Now look up from the petals of the Rose Temple, look up into the heavens and see…. What do you see? Look beyond the spheres immediately surrounding the earth. Look up to your future in that world of infinite harmony and beauty and love....

Let us now leave the temple and enter the sunlit golden garden of roses to inhale the lovely soft air. Breathe in the fragrance of the roses ... absorb it into your being. Feel the fragrance. As you breathe in the fragrance it will pass through your being and it will heal you, purify you and raise you up from darkness to light. It will refresh you when you are tired and comfort you when you are sad. It will help you to bring healing to the world of nature.

Rest here for a little ... relaxed, loved, at peace, in communion with the earth.

Divine Flames

White Eagle remembers Native American days.
Go back in memory to the times when we all assembled in a large circle, sitting upon Mother Earth and watching the campfire burning in our midst. As we sat, we inhaled the perfumes of the earth and the pines and the flowers and the woods.

Picture all our brethren gathered in the hush of the evening, listening to the orchestra of nature—the wind in the pines and the murmur of the insects and faint twitter of birds and furry beasts, beaver and rat and all the tiny beasts of water and wood—all one great happy brother–sisterhood, living under the protection and by the love of the invisible power, the Great White Spirit, all gathered around the flames.

> *The fire burns in our midst, the golden fire, emitting flames, the flames of creation.*

Do not let these fires sink away again into the earth. Yours is the heritage, and yours is the opportunity, to keep these campfires burning. The power of the fire is our power, and it is all power. It is creative power, it is life, it is of God. It is the divine and the ancient fire of the Great Spirit. Love is the fire, the great life force.

If you let yourselves go into the light of the spirit and the power of the heavens, you will feel the warmth, like a glowing fire in your heart. This is the source of all physical healing. This is the Great White Light that was used in the temples of the holy mysteries. This Great White Light is the secret of creation. It is the power which alone can control and overcome all darkness on earth. You can keep that flame burning once it has been lighted. Think of millions of flames lighting the earth. You may be only one little one, but keep the light of your flame burning!

Always look to the light, always absorb the light, and in your thoughts always give forth light. Commence with your own loved ones, and then extend your giving to all humanity and to all nature, to animals and birds and all forms of life. Send forth the light and warmth from the sacred fires of creation which are placed in your own being and which rise to your heart and head. There are many forms of service in your world, but this service of the light, this quickening of the vibrations of the planet, is a rare service and brings a great blessing to all of you on earth.

Even in giving your hand in friendship to the one by your side, give forth through your hand the warmth of the Divine Fire that is in your being. It is in these fires of life that we all live. Within you, within each individual, is a spark of divine life. As this light, this spark, grows into a flame and eventually into a great fire, beyond the physical plane this attunement reaches into the spheres of spirit life around the earth. It extends beyond and beyond into the cosmos, into the great infinite and eternal life which ranges far beyond your own solar system.

From your solar system and all the planets and the stars, you go beyond into other systems of life. Yet you, the tiny spark, are linked with all life—throughout space, into eternity.

Prayers of the Flame

Great Spirit of Love! Pour down upon us, Thy children, Thy glorious light, that our eyes may be illumined, touched with the divine fire and light, to see the beauty of all things. May we receive even now the baptism of holy fire; may we be illumined with the wisdom of the spirit. Amen.

O Great Spirit, may the divine fire within our hearts rise up! May we be filled with love and compassion, gentleness and kindness for all who walk beside us on life's journey—human beings, animals and all the companions of the nature world. We thank Thee for the wondrous blessing that we have received. Amen.

Visualization

Close your eyes. Close your senses to the outer world, and imagine that we are all sitting around a campfire under a starlit sky with the brother–sisterhood of nature. In incarnations past we all sat round this fire, and from the fire we felt a warmth which penetrated our hearts. We were raised up in spirit as the sparks of the fire floated upwards…. We were all carried up into heavenly heights.

Let us do that now. Through our imagination, through imagining the sense of smell, the sense of touch, through the sense of hearing and the sense of taste and sight on the etheric plane, let us contact nature here—around our campfire. Concentrate upon that fire which is in our midst, and see the light and the sparks, which represent human hearts … divine sparks in every human heart, all rising from that one central fire.

The sparks all gather together high in the heavens, and you will see that there is a star forming. There is now, blazing in our midst, a spiritual Star which is beyond all earthly description.

This life that you create when you live consciously—or this good that you make real on earth—goes forth, and the light itself forms this blazing Star. On the invisible plane the light speeds forth and the healing of the earth goes on.

You are part of that Star when you think of it, and you think of the little divine spark that you are. You join all the other little sparks from that fire, as they form a blazing Star.

It is a continually blazing fire. The flames are leaping from this Star which you, by your love, create. Feel it … meditate upon it…. We are in the blazing Star… We see this Star pouring its light over the whole earth….

FROM FIRE TO EARTH: *Sunlight on the Mountains*

Let us rise together to the mountaintops…

Visualize the vast snow-capped peaks bathed in the golden sunlight. Hear the word of power, the creative word, resounding through the mountains—OM…. OM…. OM…. on and on and on. From that creative sound, all life comes forth and to it all life returns; it is the source of all your inspiration and strength and joy; the source of all your power to work with and serve your fellow beings.

We are all in touch with this infinite strength … it is truth…. It is the ancient wisdom. Comparatively few on earth attune themselves to that power, or even give it a thought: but just think, beloved, what it can mean to a life, to any life, to your life! How blessed you are to be continually in touch with that centre of blazing light and infinite life-force!

Unveil that light, and what you have received give again; which also means, give on all planes to a work which is born of the spirit and serves the human spirit, for if those who have passed from your vision had not given, you would not now be receiving. Make it possible for many, many, many souls to receive that light which has come to be a precious thing to you in your life.

Let us rise in thought, in spirit, right up into the mountaintops.

EARTH HEALER

CHAPTER SIX

Earth: Holy Mountains

THERE ARE a number of holy mountains in different parts of the earth. It is noticeable how frequently the mountaintop is referred to in connection with the masters. Think for a moment about this. It is natural to go up a mountain to seek light, to seek peace; you want to raise your consciousness away from the plains, away from the depths. To the heights you naturally aspire, and so you think of the centre of holiness as on a mountain.

In our Native American life, we used to repair to the mountains, climbing quite high to sit in meditation and to watch the rising and the setting of the sun. In the golden light we were surrounded by the perfection of natural life, and we would not leave our post until we had an answer to our prayer. We did not attempt to solve our problems in the noise of the camp life, but rose to the mountaintop—the mountain of the higher consciousness, as well as the physical mountain.

To 'repair to the mountaintop' is a raising of your consciousness to a plane above the material, above the world of darkness. For the earth plane is the plane of darkness, and the earth planet is the darkest planet. Yet even the darkest planet can become light, and the day will come when the atoms of the earth will change. They will gradually evolve into a state of light and beauty. We bring you peace and love, and would raise you to a world above the earth plane.

So we raise our consciousness; we journey to the mountaintop, in the way spoken of in the book of Isaiah: 'Get thee up into the high mountain'. That mountain is the higher consciousness, not confined to the centre in the head, but expanding beyond the physical limitations. Come with us to the mountaintops.

See for yourselves the grandeur and the glory of this scene with the mountain peaks around you. These peaks are symbols of the Great Ones, the great masters of all time, who have brought so much love and help to struggling humanity. Remember that without this loving service from the great masters and their assistants, the angelic powers, humanity would by now be extinct.

May the brotherhood of all life sing in your souls! As we rise to the mountaintop to gaze upon the golden sun on the horizon, we know eternal peace and at-one-ment. We know that our feet are set upon a path which will lead unfailingly to the eternal happiness we seek.

Prayers on the Mountaintops

We worship the Great Architect of the Universe. We bow our heads in simple humility before His works. May we all be receptive to His love, to His wisdom and to His beauty. May we learn patience; may we understand true simplicity; and through these qualities may we construct within our being the great temple of Light. Amen

O Great White Spirit, we thank Thee for our creation and for the glories which lie before us. May we learn to walk patiently and serenely along the path of life with joy singing in our hearts, and praises on our lips for Thy love and blessing. Amen.

We pray to the source of life and truth, wisdom and love, for understanding and for peace; and we humbly pray that we may rise to the mountaintops as we quietly attune with the spirit life. There we call to our brethren in the angelic realms to direct to the earth the rays of divine love, intelligence and peace. Amen.

Visualization

Will you go once more to the mountain heights? Together, let us visualize the snow, and in that light we see all the colours of the spectrum.

Enter into the great, deep silence and peace, here in the quiet and lonely places. You are far removed from the chattering crowds…. Will you now visualize the holy mountain before you?

See this vast mountain rising above you, rising to the greatest heights! On the apex of that mountain, see the golden Star Temple blazing, pulsating with light. Watch it sending out rays of light, reaching beyond the range of your vision. The glory of that light which falls on the snow-capped mountain is from heaven.

We leave you, up in the spiritual spheres where the Grand Master stands with hands upraised in blessing, and where the great masters—illumined by the light, clothed in light—stand. The mountains encircle the whole company…. As we withdraw, gently, you feel the stillness, the purity, the holiness….

Divine Mother

The ancients worshipped the sun, the giver of life, and earth, the Divine Mother, who receives into her womb the life-germ. The mother receives and unfolds only to give forth in more mature form the life of God: Divine Mother is the spirit of creation, the spirit of giving. Yet while Divine Mother is creating and giving forth life, she is also withdrawing life. She does not destroy; she gives forth from the womb of wisdom and she withdraws into the heart of love. The true mother does not possess: she releases, she gives freedom and understanding and sympathy and help. Divine Mother is the manifestation of the universal spirit of birth and life and death.

The Divine Mother is also the embodiment of motherhood, drawing close to all men and women, to succour, aid and strengthen them. She comes to love them and protect them and to use them to help humanity by pouring forth in the world eternal love. This Mother Spirit is the giver of life, the protector of the seed of life in the womb of life; she is the spirit of mothering those who are sad and sick and weary, estranged and lonely; those who feel irritation and weariness. This includes feeding and clothing the people, physically and spiritually. It means healing the nations. This spirit of divine as well as physical motherhood is almost the greatest thing in life.

Do not some of you also feel the need for that Mother's love? Is not the world longing for such a love? Does not humanity everywhere seek the Great Mothering Spirit? The kingdom of nature is thirsting for this, that spirit of divine motherhood and that gentle love and wisdom which rules all life. Picture her manifesting not only through physical form, but as the Divine Mother in all nature—as the Mother Earth, producer of all life, beauty, purity and sweetness, and of the food so bountifully given to sustain the human race. You could not live without the bounty of Divine Mother. Try to feel a sense of thankfulness which will develop into worship and adoration of this supreme love and power. There is so much to fill you with happiness.

This is what we all did in the past: we all

When you have been able to attune yourselves to the Great Mother-Soul of the earth planet, you will have felt that inflow of love and compassion for all life.

found this sweet and wonderful happiness. We were happy; we were spontaneously joyful because we enjoyed simple things: the clear starlit nights, the trickling waters, the wind in the trees, the perfume of the flowers in the woods. We loved our friends, the song of the birds and the beautiful colours. All these things made us happy. They were the gifts of a wise mother, the Wise Mother, the giver of life, beauty, happiness; and even when you see what you call tragedy and sorrow, you can be sure that the wise mother is leading her child from self-interest and self-ishness and errors to that beautiful land of joy and perfection. She would lead us all to the true land of happiness.

Prayers to Divine Mother

Let us turn to the Great Mother, the Divine Mother—all love, all wisdom. In thought and in soul, we rise into the heavenly spheres. We rise into the infinite and eternal garden, and offer our grateful hearts to the Divine Mother, giver of the physical form of life. We bow our heads in adoration. Amen.

Divine Mother God, we thank Thee for the outpouring of Thy love upon us all. May we be gathered to Thy breast and find Thy peace. May Thy care and compassion bless and heal this planet. Amen.

Now let us lift our eyes once more. Great Mother Nature, we worship Thee, we reverence Thee and we long to grow closer to Thee and to raise all our fellow creatures up into Thy heavenly state and Thy peace. May Thy peace shine in the heart, dwell in the heart of every one of Thy children on this planet earth. Amen.

Visualization

In the ancient days, even before there were stone temples, the simple brethren congregated on a high plain or hilltop; and although trees are not frequently found at such a height, we are taking you to a temple of trees. The trees that you see are immense, like pillars of verdant green. You will see the tall aisle or nave which is built from the sweeping, graceful branches of the trees, and the light of the spiritual sun shining on to the leaves which move gently in the breeze. In that sunlight, if you look very closely with your heart as well as your higher mind, you will see the countless forms of the sun spirits and the little sylphs in the gentle breeze.

You become aware of how the trees form a natural temple. It was because of such natural temples created by the great Mother Nature that, at a later time, the idea of building in stone came to humankind.

We want you to see now in your imagination this same temple in the heavens: a pure, natural structure of the graceful trees and the myriad spirits of the sun and the air, and the earth—the spirits of the earth rising from the earth and becoming active on the green carpet which covers the arena. Meditate here on this, get the feeling of the Brotherhood, the Brotherhood which has been in existence beyond the calculation of the human mind, millions of years ago. Get the feeling of this brotherhood of life—hear the song of the birds, smell the sweetness of all nature here in this temple.

We want everyone to see with clear vision what is taking place in the temple. You see Mother Earth rising too with the soul of the earth, and you see the manifestation of her beauty in the budding and the opening of the leaves and the flowers, in the sweet fragrance of the earth. You see the Mother Divine rising in physical form and turning her face towards the sun. Divine Mother, all love and wisdom, harmony and beauty; it is she who gives life and form to the earth!

Heavenly Gardens

O brethren, in our life on earth, in the woods and by the running river where we lived with our people, we found that intense peace and happiness which you in your present life so often miss.* The Native Americans talked to the spirit of the trees, and the flowers, to the running water. They talked to the Great Spirit in the mountains—all life was the Great White Spirit to them.

We advise you, when you are troubled in mind, to walk in your garden, walk over the soft turf, and to look at the blades of grass ... they are part of you because you are part of God, you are part of the sun. You could not live without the sun, or the water, or the air, or the earth; nor can you live spiritually without bridging the etheric gap by the senses of your soul.

When you enter what we describe as the infinite and eternal garden, and visit your own particular section of that garden, you look at the flowers, the birds and the tiny leaves shooting from the stem; you feel an intense love and thankfulness for this manifestation of the Creator's love for all creation. In thinking along these lines, your thoughts come from your heart more than from your brain; the heart holds thoughts of infinite, tender love; the feeling of becoming part of all this creation.

Walk in the garden and you will see evidence of God's love and God's beauty, God's gentleness. You will see how nature is gradually unfolding. It seems as though there is an uprush of light and love which is reaching out to you—to you, my brother and my sister, telling you how you are loved by your Creator who has placed you in this beautiful world, and on this green and beautiful earth. So, my children, sink back and rest in the everlasting arms which are around you. Make your choice to follow the Star, the Spirit, the Sun, which goes out into the world to help in the purification of the whole world, the purification of the soil and all the elements. You, who love the earth and all growing things, can make your contribution to the growth and beauty by loving and co-operating with the

> *May your imagination reveal to you the gardens of the spirit.*

*This paragraph and the next also appear in the book WHITE EAGLE ON FESTIVALS AND CELEBRATIONS.

nature kingdom.

Oh, what a wonderful life we see, with all beings living together in harmony and enjoyment of life! This is as the Garden of Eden was and will be—for as above, so below. Take heart, take courage, dwell in the light and nurture the Star of light and warmth deep within your being.

You may yet be standing in a garden filled with flowers, perfume, music; you may hear the song of the birds, and the wind in the trees. Ask, seek, knock, and the door shall be opened unto you and life will become full of joy and promise!

Prayers in the Heavenly Garden

O Gracious Spirit: to our brethren in the spheres of light, to our beloved ones in spirit, to all the nature kingdom, to all the animal kingdom, we give thanks, praise and love; and in this vast brotherhood of life may we know the peace of Thy spirit brooding over all life. Amen.

Almighty and beloved Father and Mother God, we thank Thee for our life and for Thy creation. We thank Thee for our vision—our sight, our hearing, our sense of touch and smell. Without these senses of the body, O Lord, we could not enjoy the blessings of Thy creation in nature and see them in the skies above; we could not enjoy the blessings of the earth, the sight of flowers and trees; we could not feel the sweetness of wind and rain; nor could we enjoy the companionship of lesser brethren, the animals and birds and all the kingdom of nature.

O Great White Spirit, we are thankful for Thy manifold blessings. Amen.

Visualization

We are taken into a green parkland. Come with us, and walk on the velvety turf of this lovely estate, breathing into your tired bodies the vibrations of health and power and buoyancy which are here…. Be recharged as we walk on this green carpet….

Life abounds; on all the blooms, on the bushes and in the trees, the little fairies are at work. You may hear the birds singing in praise and thanksgiving for their life. You see the soft green trees, perfect in grace, in colour and in perfume. We catch the voice of each tree, speaking to our soul of the love and beauty of God's life, and find in each tree a brother or a sister who is in harmony with our own heart. We see the form and life which the great Mother brings. Yet we see not only the forms of the trees, but the forms of angels behind these trees, and we know that there is intelligent life in nature. The trees are in their spring dress—the springtime, a time of promise. Do you see the flowering shrubs, the blazing colours in this massed group of flowers?

*

We look about the gardens and we see spreading plants and growing vines, beautified by the flowers which their work has produced. We see a carpet of flowers, and we see also the soft blanket of green grass. We hear the song of the birds and the lowing of cattle, the murmur of the voices of the animals. We hear the hum of bees. We listen to the singing of birds, the language of our animal brethren, and the music of the flowers—which comes to our senses as perfume and colour.

The air is full of the music of insect, bird and beast, and flower and tree, and we know that we are part of all this grand life, and the beauty of these things inspires us with a great longing, with a great love, to give this joyous experience to all humanity. The waving grasses invite us to rest … and we rest….

FROM EARTH TO AIR: *A Tree in Starlight*

We would share with you* a vision that has come so clearly as we have been doing our work this evening—the vision of a most beautiful tree. It was a great tree, so tall and strong. The trunk rose to quite a height, and the branches spread nearly beyond our sight. It almost became a tree of light, and yet it was still a beautiful, natural tree such as we see growing from Mother Earth, lifting its branches towards the sky. But as I gazed upon this tree, I saw the people of all nations being drawn together, coming together in peace and brotherhood under the protection of the branches of that tree…

And it was not only men and women, the people of all nations, all faiths (my attention was drawn particularly to this—men and women of all faiths and all races) but also the animal kingdom coming together in peace and harmony under that beautiful tree. And I saw birds perched among the branches of the tree, and the birds were singing…. It was a vision of peace and a vision of joy.

Then I saw that above this great tree, the Star was shining.

*These words were given at an evening meeting in the White Eagle Lodge, but are not by White Eagle himself.

The Native Americans who worshipped the Great White Spirit worshipped the whole creation of Almighty Being; they gazed at the sky with thankfulness and recognized the power that existed in the sky. They recognized it in the stars and the planets, in the sun and the moon—for they knew that the planets and stars had a great influence over the earth and over their own lives.

CHAPTER SEVEN

Air: Wide Skies

YOU HAVE already learned about some of the ceremonies of the past, where the peoples gathered together during the night to perambulate their temple—which was a level place set in the midst of mountains. There the ancient brethren paced their vast concourse, which lay under the open sky, lit by myriad stars. Looking up to the canopy of heaven, they gazed upon the stars' twinkling light, which represented more to them than just little lights in the sky…. It meant those powers of God which can destroy and recreate. The light from other planets, both seen and unseen, fell gently upon the vast gathering. Even as they gazed up into the heavens, to the twinkling lights there, the stars spoke to their innermost hearts of love, of brotherhood, of peace…. All present understood that they were worshipping under the direction of the angels of the light.

Think of the heavens now, of the deep blue canopy above you, and see the stars shining in that canopy of the heavens. As you gaze into the night sky, open your heart without fear…. Look into the heavens and see the host of stars, each one of them a creation of the Great Spirit.

Now let us rise away from earth to the temple of the great white light in the heavens. In this temple, which is open to the heavens (for it is canopied by universal space, in which we see stars shining, stars which were once planets like your earth but which have now passed far beyond the density of the earth), we become aware of the harmony of the spiritual worlds in which the higher part of our being, our soul, lives.

Do not depend upon anyone else for your happiness. See it everywhere shining like the stars that twinkle out of the deep blue sky at night. In little things happiness comes. Happiness comes to you in all the simple things; and even in a city you can always look up to the sky and feel the wonderful hum of continual life, and look beyond the rooftops to see the stars. This will help you to understand how you, as a star, can give light as in a dark sky at night.

EARTH HEALER

Prayers of the Starlit Sky

Beloved ones … in consciousness may we be raised onto the hillside, with the canopy of the blue skies above us, and may we feel the beauty, the peace and the eternal love of our Father God. May we be inspired with courage, with faith, to travel the path towards the eternal peace. May each one present go forth from this place conscious of the companionship of guardian angel, guide, and teacher; and may each one know that all is well … all is love. Amen.

Let us in spirit worship God in silence under the heavenly canopy of stars; let us commune with the spirits of the air and the fire and the water and the beautiful earth. The peace of the eternal love and harmony fills our being; our eyes are opened to the glorious presence of the Perfect One and the vast company of heaven…. We receive Thy blessing with humble thankfulness. Amen.

Visualization

We stand on the hilltop, amid trees and air, with the stars above … and we are conscious of peace of soul…. The stars shine through the deep blue canopy, and the sun and the moon together blend their light.

As the first streaks of dawn become visible, a great hush falls, a great stillness. Expectantly and silently waiting, we watch the sun rising in the east. As the sun slowly rises over the horizon, we look out from the mountain heights, and look upon the scene of humanity's travail.

We see the glorious healing rays of light pouring upon the earth. We see peace restored—a much greater, deeper peace than the world has known during the whole of this present cycle….

We turn to the light, worshipping, praising, thanking the Great White Spirit for the coming of the new day.

Angel Wings

As Native Americans we learned a little of how to make contact with the angelic brotherhood, who are still our silent helpers, and are the controllers and directors of natural forces like the winds and the rain. Remember that when a person can see and recognize the presence of angels, he or she is tuning in to the infinite spiritual power. These angels are powerful beings, and when we send forth peace and goodwill, not merely by word of mouth but from the substance of our spirit, we are causing the angels to be drawn once again into our midst, as the thought power of humans is a real, living and vibrating force in the world of spirit.

The great angels of the elements have the natural world in their care.

We would draw your attention to the presence of angels on your planet. We want to open your consciousness to the importance of working with the angelic kingdom. Speak to your good angels, national angels, those angel beings who are over your country; appeal to them, seek their power and their love. They will serve you in purity; they work dispassionately. They have a great deal to do with the spiritual evolution of humanity, and in this present period of the earth's development you will find much greater angelic power will be in evidence on your planet, stimulating the heart centre of the earth itself. Ask the angels, seek the co-operation of the angels that live entirely to serve God, the Great White Spirit and humanity, your brothers and sisters all over the world.

We see the angels working with the substance we give them, so that forms of peace and goodwill live among humanity, until they have served the purpose for which they are created. We find this universal brother–sisterhood, this community of people and of angels, is continually being welded together and strengthened. There can be no separation between angels and humanity; they work together side by side.

Call upon the angels and you will know where the key to the gate of Heaven is to be found; you will know how to insert that key and unlock the gates. You will be the companions of the angelic brotherhood who are ready to lift the veil and show you the very deepest secrets of nature and of creation and of the life-forces in the earth, in the rocks, in the water, in the fire, in the air.

Imagine that we are gathered together on a mountain height, with blue stars like jewels in the sky … and you are able to see hosts of angels, perhaps not as clearly as human forms, but in the white mists with the golden light of the heavens shining through. In the apparent clouds you will see angel forms, winged beings. The reason why they appear to you and to many others as winged is because they are sending out currents of heavenly light and power. These currents go out in the form of circles; it is just like a fountain of light and life-force. This the angels send to you, and you can be receptive if you attune yourselves to these angels.

Now peace be with you all. The great Angel of Peace is in your midst, the great white wings of love are enfolding you. Peace, peace be with you. Remember, white wings encompass you.

Prayers of the Angels

As the angels draw near and bless us with their peace, we raise our hearts to the Infinite, the divine spirit of love, and we thank God for our creation, our preservation and all the joys and beauties of the world. Amen.

We pray for a greater understanding of the glories of creation. We open our hearts in love and adoration to the Great Ones in the angelic world, praying that they may draw very close to our waiting hearts, and that we may not hear the words alone, but hear with the hearing of the spirit, hear with the inner perception—that we may listen with the hearing of the spirit within. We pray that we may understand how to give ourselves in greater measure to the great plan of evolution. And in humility of spirit we wait for the light. Amen.

O Great Spirit, we earnestly pray that each soul may receive the blessing of Thy love and wisdom. May all receive a manifestation of the power and the presence of the angels of the Christ circle. We pray that the light may go forth to cover the whole earth. May the angels' song of peace and goodwill to all people become a reality in the soul of humankind. Amen.

Visualization

Leaving behind all earthly things, will you come with us above the earth just as if you were flying on wings through space? Come with us to a realm in the highest heights, and imagine yourself above the earth in the temple of the Star. It is immense … all around you is tier upon tier of shining spirits; a vast company who are working with you to send out healing light to purify and beautify the planet earth.

In the quietness, aspire to become aware of the angelic presences all around you; strive to hear the music of their love, and to see the glory of the colours. You will see the most delicate colours of the rainbow, moving, vibrating, in beautifully soft, billowy clouds; and see beings standing with folded wings all around. Their robes are sparkling, scintillating, and in these little specks of light you will see all the colours of the spectrum, all the colours of the sun.

Now, in the centre of the group we see the planet earth. There you will see all the immensity of nature spread before you. Perfect landscape, golden-crested mountains, great trees…. Look! You will see a cross going round the planet from north to south, and east to west. You will see the planetary angels all around, and countless souls in the very centre and heart of the earth and the cross. You will see the rays of colour from those great planetary angels falling on the earth. Then you will see the great angels of the elements. You will see them pouring the sun's rays; then you will see the gentle rain falling from the air, and water spirits and the angels of earth bringing those people sustenance for their physical bodies and their souls.

A deep hush falls … and all the angels fold their wings, and stand in silent worship.

Thy peace, O Gracious Spirit, we feel, and we thank Thee for our creation, and for the creation of our world. Amen.

The angels are still … They are not disturbed by any world problem: they know one truth, that all is working together for good. They come to help humanity realize this one grand truth … *that all is working together for good.* You have nothing, nothing to fear. God is with you and has given his angels charge over you.

Winds of Heaven

The Native American brothers studied the ways of nature, studied the wind currents and the rain clouds and the four seasons. They recognized that behind all these natural forces there was a directing power with which they could work in harmony. This power works not only on the mental and spiritual planes, but it works right through to the physical level of life.

You are at the beginning of the new Aquarian Age, and old, outworn, constricting habits of thought and life are being broken down. Now there is a particularly powerful wind sweeping over the globe. It is as though a beautiful fresh wind is blowing through the earth, and it is the work of all to think goodness, and to trust God and God's laws—which are just, perfect and true.

Be at peace, but do your best by thinking constructively, and remember always that most valuable lessons are being learned. You are now on the cusp of the Aquarian Age and there is so much in the old Piscean Age which is as chaff, and must be swept away. The great Angel of Air is blowing away all that is not wanted. When you hear the wind, rejoice that it is the breath of God, the power of the Angel of the Air sweeping away the chaff to lead you on a golden path to a new way of life.

The winds of heaven will sweep clean the pathway of the New Age.

We are only concerned with the spiritual evolution, the goodness, the happiness, the peace of all God's children on earth and in the spheres surrounding the earth. Earthly people live with a kind of barrier all around them. You must get rid of that barrier, which is like a dense fog. The only thing that can disperse fog apart from sunlight is the winds of heaven.

A great light burns within you. You are the only person who can uncover that light and turn it up in strength, causing it to shine brightly so that the fogs of earth are dispersed. You can generate a power, too, in yourselves that, like the winds of heaven, will sweep clean your surroundings until all mists disappear.

Prayers of the Wind's Path

Deep peace of the open prairie and the wind-swept sky, the flowing rivers and quiet valleys and the noble trees which raise their heads to Thee in adoration and praise, standing stalwart and true on the mountainside, steady through all the boisterous winds of life … may the peace of God dwell within us, giving unto us a like strength, to bring us back to Thee, our Father. Amen

We lift our hearts to the hills and to the mountains, and feel all around us the beauty and power of nature. We worship the grandeur and glory of our Creator's handiwork and, becoming in tune with the infinite Spirit, we awaken to the beauty within ourselves. We yearn to become united in fuller consciousness with the glory of God our Father; and in this grand brotherhood may we learn to fold to our breasts our brethren of the human and animal kingdoms. May all fear leave us, and may we know love, and beauty, and peace. Amen.… Amen.

Visualization

Can you recall the reaction upon your feelings or soul body when you first listened to the wind in the trees…? When you hear that sound, do you reach out and touch something not purely physical, not only some vibration of the air?

How did music originate? We would say, by an effort to reproduce the sounds in the air created by the winds. Listen now to the wind in the tree-tops and imagine you are hearing heavenly music … hearing the music of the creative life….

And as you attune your hearing to these vibrations of sound, and reach behind the physical to the inner hearing, you will hear the mysterious word, the great Word of Power, the creative Word, pervading the air….

We pray to enter into the grand orchestra of life's harmony and perfection. May we be ever prepared to hear the voice of the wind speak through all nature like music. The music that is coming will raise the vibrations of the earth.….

FROM AIR
TO WATER:
*The Wind
and the
Rain*

We worship the grandeur and glory of our Creator's handiwork, and, becoming in tune with the infinite Spirit, we awaken to the beauty within ourselves.

Do you feel the peace and the beauty of the spirit spheres? Yes? Now breathe in the breath, the air of the spirit…. The music of the wind breathes its message to heart and mind. We lift our hearts to the hills, to the mountains, to the wind-swept skies, to the rain-drenched earth, to the beauty and power of nature. The great angel of water is ministering to humanity, ministering to the earth.

*All the world is
thirsting for the
living waters—
for truth.*

CHAPTER EIGHT

Water: Mighty Oceans

YOU ARE standing on the shore looking out over a vast ocean, preparing to journey across that ocean. Your deep need is to be able at all times to catch the voice of the Spirit across the ocean of turmoil and conflict; to feel and inhale the beauty and the truth of life.

Sit in the silence and you will hear secrets whispered to you. Go out into the sunlit dawn with the sea rolling upon the shore beneath you, and listen with your heart, and you will hear secrets whispered to you again; secrets of which it is quite impossible to speak, but which come to you only in your heart. Our earthly comprehension reels with the magnificence of the stillness and power of the sea.

May the ocean speak to you of the eternal powers that lie within the creation of the universe; the waters enfold humanity in an enveloping yet impersonal peace … in the grasp of an immense power. Truth is like the ocean, rhythmic and irresistible. The sea may lie still and quiet … and standing alone in some quiet place, the soul can reach out and become conscious of the vastness, the depth and the profundity of life.

You will know how things happen, why things happen and how evolution is proceeding. The sands beneath the sea, like the great oceans, are built up from tiny units; the whole universe has been created—and is still being created—from the tiny atom. You are specks in the ocean; you are grains of sand on the shore. Your little personality is a drop in the great ocean. The unit must become completely absorbed into the whole while still retaining its individuality, like the grain of sand on the shore. Each grain is essential, each drop in the ocean is essential, but all are separate. Few have got as far as developing the self into the selfless. Be strong in the self, but be stronger in the selfless.

The earth can be battened down, as it were, into the hold of a great ship. You must glimpse the beauty of the ocean through which that ship is ploughing its way—onward, onward, onward into the light; while above you is a blazing Star linked to your heart.

Unveil the Star, projec-

ting light and love supreme from your heart—and realize that there are millions of angels working with you. Together you project this brilliant, blazing Star, the Christ Star. You project this over the seas, to cleanse ... to heal the earth and the waters alike.

Prayers of the Ocean

O Gracious Spirit, eternal Light, we pray to be so purified by the expression of Thy love in our hearts that vision of the eternal mysteries may be permitted us. May the oceans of the spirit bring cleansing and healing to our earth, clearing the mists and allowing us to glimpse eternal life. Amen.

Gracious Spirit of love, we thank Thee for the beauty which we find in life, in the spirit world, and on this earth plane, and in the hearts of humanity. We thank Thee for the companionship of the great open spaces, and of the sky, and of the running water and the roaring sea; for the quiet wonder of earth. And for Thy blessing, O God, we thank Thee.... Amen.

Visualization

We are taking you to a temple which is built by the angels of the sea, the angels of the marine life. See that your temple is like the interior of a most beautiful shell. Feel yourselves in this enormous and beautiful shell in the sea. See the marine life, see the beauty of the plants and shells and all the life that you know (and life that you do not know) which exists in the sea. Extend your vision to the etheric sea, feel it and see it. There is a marvellous beauty in the shell temple.

Now you go back, back, back into the past.... See, you are part of it, you are in the body of a fish swimming in the ocean. You see you are all part of this whole universe. Go to it, live in it, be it ... the universal life of ocean as well as land, as well as sky and the higher ether. You are in the whole of life.

We learn also that as we become at one with this great harmony of life nothing can hurt or despoil the pure whiteness of God's spirit working in our souls. We seek no earthly protection ... there is none. We find the waters of peace and the sunshine and joy of life. We take nothing. We give ... we give ... we give.

Clear, Still Pools

If you look into still water, you will see a clear reflection of yourself—or of anything else in the picture. If you look into water that is stirred up and troubled, you will see a distorted reflection. By this simple illustration you learn the necessity of control and calmness of mind if you are going to see truth. Truth will only be revealed when there is stillness and peace. You must have that stillness if you would reflect truth. In your meditation you may possibly see a pool or lake with lotus flowers upon its surface. Since water symbolizes the emotions, you learn from this scene that the emotions have to be stilled and controlled if healing is to begin.

A lake or a pool of water is a symbol of complete stillness. When still, it reflects the divine.

Imagine you are seated at the lotus pool. The water represents your soul or psyche, the lilies represent the chakras in your soul, and the Star above you represents the Great Spirit. That Star must shine down and be reflected in your soul. When you aspire to the Star, its light and form is reflected in your soul and in your character and eventually in your physical body.

Now lay aside that active brain. Quieten it down by the aspiration of your spirit, working through your heart as well as through the lotus of the crown, so that you may be united in the higher mental and spiritual spheres. Do you feel the power immediately flowing into you from the still pool? Conserve that power, that life-force, that energy. Learn to conserve the spiritual power. We are thinking at this moment of the great need your earth has for the kind of help that the light projected from your heart can give to the whole world. It is a question of pouring into a central pool or reservoir as much light as the human soul can give out.

In your daily work, however material it may appear to be, let it be a song of praise and thanksgiving as you surrender to God, and in this state the human spirit will find that peace of the still pool which the world cannot find—in its efforts and rush, in its desire for self-gratification in some form or another. Seek the pool, surrender to the Great Spirit, find that inner tranquillity and peace. Cultivate your observation of nature, all the kingdoms of nature. This will not only bring to you knowledge, it will bring you a deep life-force.

If you can daily make contact with this central power, the source of all life, and particularly that spiritual strength and love and beauty and happiness which can flow from the lotus pool into you and fill your being, then you will be a dynamic power for peace in the world.

Prayers of the Still Pool

O Gracious Spirit, may we be receptive to Thy blessings, responsive to the influences of love and peace that come to us from the world of nature. As we gaze into the depths of the still waters, may we be filled with the spiritual power of love and kindliness and goodwill, so that we may be pure channels of healing and help to our world. Amen.

O Gracious Spirit, in Thy presence we surrender our hearts to Thee. To all the nature kingdom, to all the animal kingdom, to the deep stillness of the lakes and mountains, we give thanks, praise and love; and in this vast brotherhood of life may we know the peace of Thy spirit brooding over all life. Amen.

Visualization

Now we are seated, not on chairs as the earthly people sit, but in the lotus position. And do you see that in the centre of our circle there is a pool of clear water? You will gaze upon the clear, still water.... We first of all see that clear pool, and on the water are the lotus blooms. The lily, the lotus, floats upon it, presenting perfect and beautiful lotus flowers. You can inhale the perfume of the flowers and the clear water.

Now meditate on this: not only the picture, but inhale as well the perfume of those white lilies; etherically inhale the perfume. It will comfort you, and you will absorb the peace, the purity of the spirit....

It is so still that those of us who are gazing into it see our reflection quite clearly. We also see the reflection of that blazing Star in the clear water.... We gaze into the golden depths of the lily, and see there the blazing Star. The rays of the Star reach right to your heart....

Now from the heart of this lily, this lotus, there shines the blazing jewel, radiating light, light, light.... Seek every morning of your life to make this contact and you will go through your day poised and happy and wise.

Crystal Waters

Let us each feel that we are lying on a beautiful green bank. There are flowers all around us and just a little beyond where we are lying there is a rippling brook. We can hear it rippling over the lovely coloured stones.... Do you hear the trickling water as it tumbles down the rocks; and do you see the nature spirits splashing and laughing in the glorious crystal water? Now this is like a little spring of clear, life-giving water, a little spring that bubbles up from the earth, and trickles down the hillside, growing broader and stronger and flowing faster sometimes as it travels, until it becomes a great river flowing onward to meet the ocean. Behold the running water trickling down from the mountainside, rushing forward, a river, towards the sea....

If you touch the water from a running brook, you touch the sparkle and the sunlight that give it life. Do you sense water only? No, more than water—an indefinable, indestructible element—you sense the very life within it, like the life of the earth. You take in a very part of the cosmic body, the life-force. As you think

> *We would liken all spiritual development to the beginning of the flowing river.*

of this, as you meditate on it, try to absorb the vibrations of all matter—mountains, stones, vibrating, pulsating with this God force; all the elements, the rain and all the water upon the earth, pulsating with this life. It is living water, the life-giver to men and women. Drink it, use it. Humankind indeed does not live by bread alone, but by all the forces of nature—all the elements and the sunlight and the air. So train yourselves to use the air, the light and the water, all to nourish you.

*

Through the water element, you can create or bring about in your physical body a surpassing harmony and peace. Think well on this. Through water can come harmony, peace.... Now it is for you to find this peace whenever you will. Even on a busy thoroughfare you can train yourself to visualize the peace and the coolness and refreshment of this water of the spirit. And thus you may carry with you the fragrance, the life-force, the blessing of health to all you meet, every day. This is the way to restore the peace of heaven on earth.

Prayers of the Crystal Waters

We raise our faces to the glory of the Sun, our Father. We worship, we glorify and pray that we may find Thee in our lives.

O Gracious Spirit, we bless and thank Thee for Thy blessing which comes as a river, a stream of golden light and refreshment perfecting our planet. Amen.

O Gracious Spirit, may we children feel the refreshment of Thy pure spirit! May the sparkling waters of truth cleanse and heal our planet. Amen.

Visualization

Here we are in the open spaces of the heavens, and here we listen to the divine orchestra, the music of the higher worlds, which tells us of the perfection of God. The music rises and falls like drops of delicate water, like a heavenly fountain....

Very close to us you may see a glimmering fountain of light.... You will feel, if you open yourself, that it is like a fountain of waterdrops, but they will be light drops falling upon you, enfolding you, refreshing you, raising you up. Imagine this baptism of music and light and power showering upon you.

Do your best to sense the purity, the music, the cleansing of this great heart of love. It is a fountain of light, of spiritual power and healing power. It is all built up by your love, your heart and the angels. It is liquid gold....

Feel it—the fountain of life! It is the healing power that can and will flow through your body to heal all nature. It is the fountain of light and power that flows through your spirit to heal broken hearts, to overcome warring, conflicting elements on the earth.

We receive the blessing of the Great Spirit through the music of the fountain, through its delicate droplets. We breathe in the perfume, we are enfolded in the glistening rainbow colours of the divine life-forces and we are blessed ... in Thy peace, O Great Spirit. Peace ... Amen.

The Source of Healing: Working with the Star

You have a most important work to do, particularly just now, in radiating the light, projecting the light. You are receiving the light within yourselves that you may be irradiated with light and give it forth to all creatures and to the planet earth. This light that you receive can be given forth through the symbol of the six-pointed Star.

This is your work in the world … look for this Star. Look for it from the mental level, and also from the physical level, because you create form by your thought; by your thought also you build your own solar body, or body of light, and this is a contribution to the solar body of the earth. Do you see the glorious Star shining down upon you?

The Star is the centre, the heart, the beginning of creation. It is the most powerful symbol there is in our world and yours. The Christ is symbolized by the Star, the perfectly balanced man or woman. This is the spirit of the cosmic Christ, the universal love. It manifests through the pure in heart, the simple, the gentle, the quiet, strong human heart. Keep

Think of the rays of creative light radiating from the Star.

your thoughts, your concentration, your life upon the Star. Live in the Star in increasing consciousness; continually, every day, think of the Star; the blazing Star, the rays from which pour down upon you and, through you, onto all life on earth.

It may help those of you who may find it difficult to concentrate if we tell you just to visualize the blazing Star, that is all. Don't think about places, names or countries, just meditate upon the blazing Star and see the rays of the Star shining out in the darkness. Put the power of the God within you behind this projection of the Star. Do not discuss the pros and cons of any problem, only see that problem in the heart of the blazing light, the Christ light. See the rays of this Star penetrating all the dark places on your earth. Think continuously, day by day, of the blazing Star; see the rays of the Star penetrate the dark places of the earth; not in your way, not in the way of the world, but by the way of God.

There is so much for you all to learn about the divine magic which lies in the centre of the

Star. Never doubt that the Star is permeating the whole of your physical life. Try and realize its power to save and to heal, and to guide you aright; to guide and to save all humanity. It represents the Christ power and the Christ life in human life. Send forth the light of the Star everywhere with love and kindness—never forcing, but gently sunning and watering the seed in the heart of humanity. Persevere with your work and you will see the slow but definite effect of the Star upon the planet. You will see the slow but steady shooting of the green plants, which are little rays of light, from the dark earth of materialism. For as nature works slowly, so does the spiritual life grow and unfold slowly and imperceptibly.

Now we take you into the Star temple. Come to the temple of the Star … the blazing Star. We are held in the very centre of the Star, in the very heart of peace and tranquillity…. See the blazing, blazing Star above the altar. Meditate on it; gaze into it, and feel the rays of light entering your heart, strengthening your spirit and your body, and illumining your mind…. We radiate love and peace to all humanity…. We are peace.

This is the beginning of the creation of another planet.

CHAPTER NINE

A Vision of the Future

WHEN A SEED is sown in Mother Earth it does not shoot up instantly. It has to mature, gradually unfold. It has to penetrate the darkness of the soil; it has to appear above the soil and then reach up to the sunlight, and in due time the glorious flower comes into bloom to give so much pleasure. Later on, when the flower has finished, then the fruit develops ... the fruit that nourishes you.

The night is passing, surely passing, and the day of joy is at hand. This earth planet, very dark at present, is slowly quickening in vibration. Take no notice of those who say that the world will never become perfect, for they are wrong. The world is destined to become an etherealized planet, a planet of perfect light; and the life on that planet will become most beautiful. Now you are aiding in the creation of a brighter world. In the same way that thought affects action, so it affects physical matter, quickening its vibration, so that eventually the whole earth will not only be beautiful to look at and to live upon. Humanity will assist in the raising of the earth planet itself, the darkness will gradually be dissolved.

We see the light bursting into the darkness. We see the light coming on earth—a beautiful flood of light and joy in your hearts, and thankfulness. We see the light, like a beautiful dawn in the very early morning, the dawning light.... We see it coming to earth, and we see the slow but sure passing of the night—the night of this winter. Remember our words:

the night *is* passing, it will just fade away with the coming sunrise. The end of the trials of the present day is in sight; then, even as the glowing sunshine which will enfold you all before very long will bless the earth, so shall you all be caught up in the warmth and light and beauty of the spirit world, the spirit life.

Humanity is ready, it is turning the scale. By its own desire for peace and goodwill, humanity is advancing, is evolving. Understand this. For life is eternal, continuously manifesting in physical form—manifesting, withdrawing, recreating. The time approaches when there will be no more self-seeking, there will be a working for the common good, for all people to advance along the path of progress on their return journey to the Great White Spirit.

So do your best quietly, patiently; but never fail to concentrate on that glorious universal creative love. Never doubt the secret of life, which is the power of love, the wisdom of love. After doing your best, rest in confidence, trusting the Great White Spirit that has created the universe....

Closing Prayer for the Earth

Let us pray for peace and healing on earth. Peace be in our hearts. May we search for wisdom: true wisdom of the spirit, the wisdom which perceives the Great Spirit working through life; which discriminates between the things that matter, the real things of life, and the unreal things that are transient, that are with us for a day and tomorrow pass into the unknown.

Let us search for the wisdom that reveals the true life of the spirit in bird and beast and flower and tree, in the stars and planets and in the great cosmic life; the wisdom that teaches that there is a purpose behind every act, behind every experience; that teaches us to live to serve life and all creatures, to serve humanity and to leave the earth plane richer for our incarnation. Amen.

A VISION OF THE FUTURE

APPENDIX

Four Processes of Healing Attunement You can Use

For all these processes, which involve a little movement and use of the breath and incorporate White Eagle's words, it is good to wear something loose and to stretch and then relax the body a little before any of these processes, if you can.

1.   A Standing Breath of Peace for Planet Earth

Find a quiet place, outside if possible, and stand with your feet firmly on the earth. If you can stand barefoot, better still. Be aware of the different parts of the sole of each foot that connect with the earth.

Loosen your knees so that you stand without locking them. Feel a relaxation that begins at the base of your spine and extends around the whole pelvic area. Let your shoulders and neck relax.

Relax fully, into the moment, and let your mind become at peace, like the surface of a still lake under the sun. The very core of your being lifts slightly as the sun warms your heart. Keep your head level so that you can breathe easily.

As you breathe, affirm:

I am a channel for healing our planet
I am at one with the earth, with the air, with the waters
I am at one with divine light, divine love, one with the sun.
With every breath I feel peace and radiate peace.

2.   *A Star Breathing Process*

Starting as before, imagine that you are standing in the clear shape of a six-pointed Star, its lower point in the earth and the upper point above your head. Its rays reach everywhere, shining out from the centre. Imagine the centre to be at your heart.

Breathe the light of the shining Star into your earthly body. As you do so, you become filled with that heavenly light. The light fills every cell of your being. You are a channel, breathing and transmitting light. Let the light go down into the earth through the soles of your feet.

Do this for six breaths.

Feel the soles of your feet at one with the earth.... Your energy reaches down into the earth. Breathe the inner spiritual fire in the heart of the earth upwards through your feet and your body to your heart. Feel this light radiating out to all life, all beings, all creation.

Do this for six breaths.

Be aware of the air and the sunlight around you. Breathe in the light that you may feel in the very atmosphere of the earth. Let it fill your being. Radiate light again from your heart into all life.

Do this for six breaths.

Affirm:

> *I am one with heaven and earth.*
> *I am full of light. I radiate light.*

3.   *Seated Among the Angels*

Sit quietly, with the back upright but not stiff. Give yourself a few minutes in preparation, relaxing your thoughts, relaxing your body, putting your emotions aside.

Let yourself remain in the quiet, steady place of your heart.

Let yourself be there in God's time, the angels' time. There visualize the Star of love, of light and healing. In the Star, your thoughts for good draw the help of the angels.

Say to yourself:

> *I seek to work in harmony with the angels of the Star to bring healing to our planet.*
> *I see the whole earth enfolded in the magical healing light of the shining six-pointed Star.*
> *I see the light of the Star shining into*
>> *the earth's soil, her plants and trees*
>> *and the animal life they support;*
>> *her streams, rivers, lakes and oceans;*
>> *her atmosphere*
> *and into*
>> *the hearts of humankind*
>> *as they walk on Mother Earth*
> *I hold in my heart and prayers the vision of planet earth cleansed, healed and in balance.*
> *May God's blessing be upon this work.*

4. *A Journey within for Healing the Earth*

Y ou may like to begin with White Eagle's prayer:

Our Brethren, we feel the life of the Great Spirit not through our mind, but through our senses, both physical and etheric. All around us are the pine trees, symbolizing peace, aspiration and strength … and the music of the wind breathes its message to heart and to mind. The Great White Spirit is brooding over all creatures … all is well.

In the spirit of this blessing, we enter our path of remembering.

I walk on Mother Earth; and by Mother Earth I am supported and nourished.

I walk beneath the canopy of the wide sky, which speaks to me also of the invisible worlds of spirit, and of the dignity of life. I draw close to the Great Spirit in my heart, to our Father–Mother God. In this presence I remember that deep within my heart is the light of the spiritual Sun, which draws heaven and earth together. The light of the Sun is within all physical form and beyond form.

Through the spiritual Sun in my heart, I offer myself in service to the angels of nature and would work with them to heal the wounds of the earth and restore balance in all her elements.

Through the creative power of the Sun, I picture the perfect form of the six-pointed star, full of light and the power for good.

I am within the Star and I see its light, with the blessing of the angels of nature, bringing healing to all the earth.…The light of the Star shines into the soil of the earth and the plants and trees it supports.…The light of the Star shines into the rivers, oceans, ice-sheets and all the waters of the earth.…The light of the Star shines into the atmosphere, the air which all creatures breathe and by which they are protected.…I see all the earth irradiated by the light and love of the Star within and around it.

The light of the Star touches the hearts and minds of humankind, to reveal a life of brother–sisterhood with the kingdoms of nature. All is held within the Star of brotherhood and peace.

As I return from this journey within, I give my thanks to the angels with whom I have prayed to co-operate. I give my thanks to the Great Spirit.

I spend a little while aware of my quiet breathing, bringing my focus outwards again to take up my outer life with joy and confidence.

May God's blessing be on this work. *Amen. Amen. Amen.*